Contents

Ship and boat safety
Ships and boats are powerful machines that travel on water. They can be very dangerous. Always have an adult with you when you look at ships and boats. Do not stand close to the water. Never go onto a ship or boat without an adult.

Ships and boats

Ships and boats are floating vehicles that carry people and things across water. Some can explore underwater. Look out for tall sailing ships and small rowing boats. Listen for the roar of motorboat engines.

You can spot ships and boats travelling on rivers, lakes, and seas. You can see them at ports and harbours. This book will help you to name the ships and boats you see. It tells you how they work. It shows you which special features to look out for.

At the back of this book is a Spotter's Guide to help you remember the ships and boats you see. Tick them off as you spot them. You can also find out the meaning of some useful words here.

Turn the page to find out all about ships and boats!

Sailing boat

Sailing boats are pushed along by the wind. Sailors move the sails to make the wind push the boat in the right direction.

A rudder helps to steer the boat left and right.

You might spot sailors leaning out of their boat. They use their body to balance the boat.

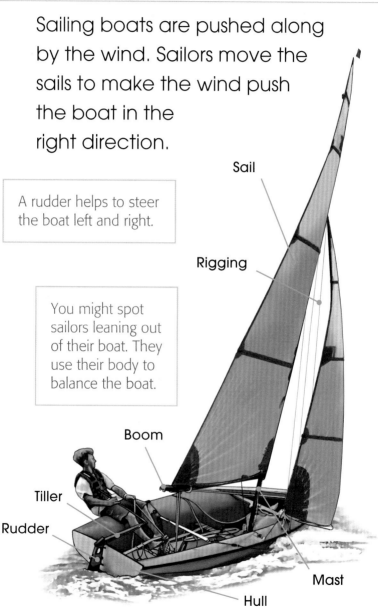

Sail

Rigging

Boom

Tiller

Rudder

Mast

Hull

Motorboat

Motorboats use engine power to move through the water. The engines turn propellers under the water.

Speedboats are very fast motorboats. They are used for fun and sport.

Steering wheel and controls

Windshield

Handrail

Outboard motor

Pointed hull shaped like a V

The propeller's blades push against the water. This pushes the boat forwards.

Fishing trawler

Trawlers catch fish by dragging huge nets through the ocean. Large fishing trawlers are floating factories.

Winches move the heavy nets around on deck.

Wheelhouse

Large hull with lots of room to store fish

They have machines for cleaning and freezing fish.

Frozen fish stay fresh. The trawler can travel further and stay at sea for longer.

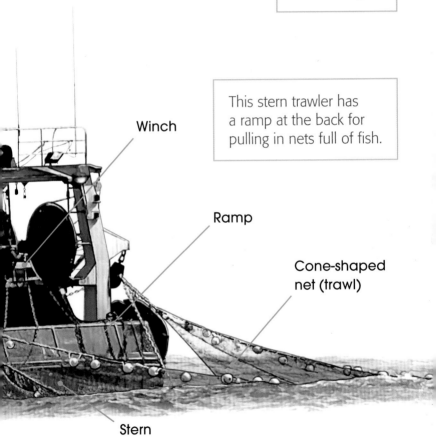

Winch

This stern trawler has a ramp at the back for pulling in nets full of fish.

Ramp

Cone-shaped net (trawl)

Stern

Canoe

This simple boat is pushed along using paddles. Canoes are used for fun, exploring, and sport. Paddlers sit or kneel on seats, facing forwards.

Kayaks are similar to canoes, but they are usually smaller and lighter.

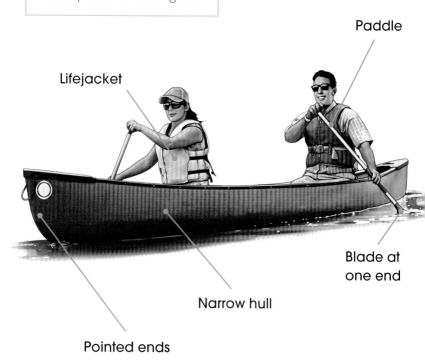

Paddle

Lifejacket

Blade at one end

Narrow hull

Pointed ends

Submarine

Submarines are boats that travel underwater. Some explore the oceans. Others work as warships. They are hard to spot. They can sneak up on other ships.

Submarines sink by letting seawater into huge tanks. They blow the water out to float up to the surface.

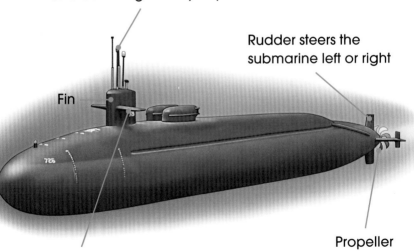

Equipment for communication and detecting nearby ships

Rudder steers the submarine left or right

Fin

Propeller

Wings help the submarine move up or down

Submarines can stay underwater for months.

Catamaran

Catamarans look like two boats joined together. Two narrow hulls travel through the water faster than one big hull. They make catamarans hard to tip over.

The deck holds the two hulls together.

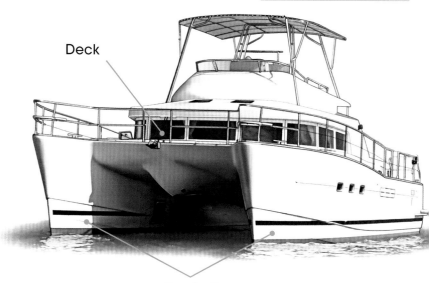

Deck

Two hulls

Many types of boat use this design. Look out for small sailing catamarans, or large ferries.

Lifeboat

Lifeboats are launched to rescue people in trouble at sea. They can speed through stormy weather and huge waves. They carry equipment to help sinking boats and treat survivors.

Smaller inflatable lifeboats are used in shallow water.

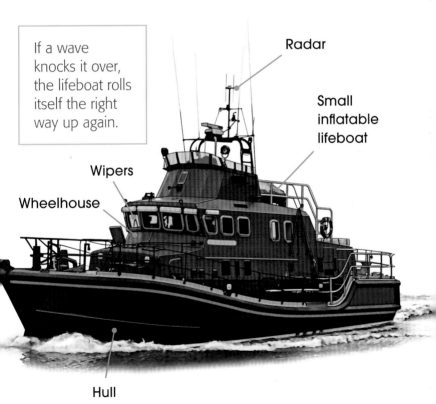

If a wave knocks it over, the lifeboat rolls itself the right way up again.

Radar

Small inflatable lifeboat

Wipers

Wheelhouse

Hull

Personal watercraft

Personal watercraft are fast and fun to ride. The best riders can perform tricks, such as back flips and rolls. They can even dive under the water.

Steering column

Personal watercraft are also known as 'Jet Skis'.

Seat

Powerful engine

Look out for lifeguards using personal watercraft to rescue swimmers.

Racing yacht

This huge yacht was built especially for racing. The crew work together to beat other boats through wind, waves, and all kinds of weather.

You can watch some races and regattas from the shore.

This America's Cup yacht can travel more than twice as fast as the wind.

Wing (sail)

The crew use winches to pull cables and position the sails.

40-metre mast

Light, strong hulls

Crew of 11 people

Traditional boat

Boats and ships have carried people and cargo over water for thousands of years. Many old designs are still used around the world.

Look out for traditional boats when you visit new places.

Punter stands at the stern

Punts can be spotted on rivers in the UK.

Pole to push boat along

Punt

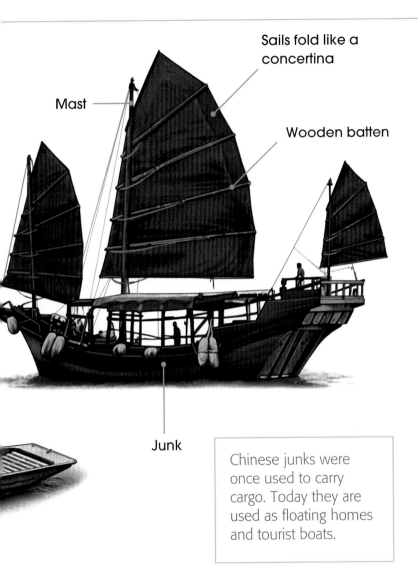

Sails fold like a
concertina

Mast

Wooden batten

Junk

Chinese junks were
once used to carry
cargo. Today they are
used as floating homes
and tourist boats.

17

 # Warship

Some warships carry equipment or soldiers to where they are needed. Others carry weapons to protect or attack targets at sea, in the air, or on land.

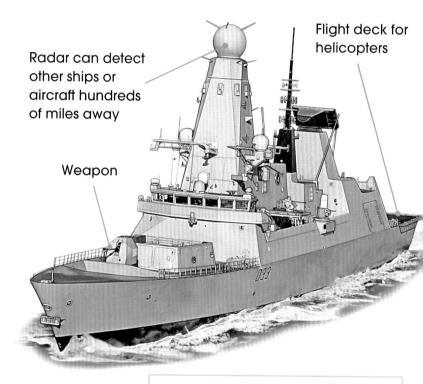

Flight deck for helicopters

Radar can detect other ships or aircraft hundreds of miles away

Weapon

This destroyer patrols the sea, looking out for trouble. It can protect other ships from aircraft attacks.

Aircraft carrier

Aircraft carriers are the biggest warships. They are floating bases for aeroplanes and helicopters. Aircraft take off and land on the huge deck.

Thousands of sailors and pilots travel onboard.

The aircraft are kept below the flight deck, and carried up by lifts.

Landing strip

Fighter plane

Flight deck

Catapult

Everything on the ship is controlled from the island

Take-off strip

Anchor

The flight deck is shorter than a normal runway. A catapult helps aeroplanes speed up quickly enough to take off.

Historic ship

Some old ships can only be seen in museums. Galleons were used hundreds of years ago. They carried cargo across the Atlantic Ocean.

Weapons protected galleons from pirates trying to steal treasure.

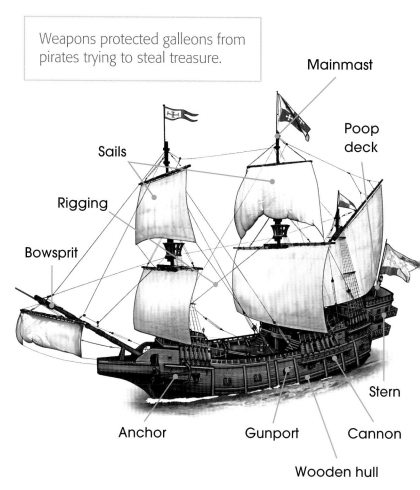

Mainmast

Poop deck

Sails

Rigging

Bowsprit

Stern

Anchor

Gunport

Cannon

Wooden hull

Inflatable boat

Inflatable boats have soft hulls made from tubes filled with air. They cost less than other boats, and are easier to store.

This whitewater raft is used for rides on fast-flowing water. Getting soaked is part of the fun.

Life jacket

Helmet

Paddle

Inflatable boat

Handle

Small inflatable lifeboats can be kept on aeroplanes and ships.

Submersible

Submersibles can dive deep underwater. They rescue damaged submarines, carry out research, and explore oceans.

Submersibles are the only way to travel to the deepest parts of the ocean.

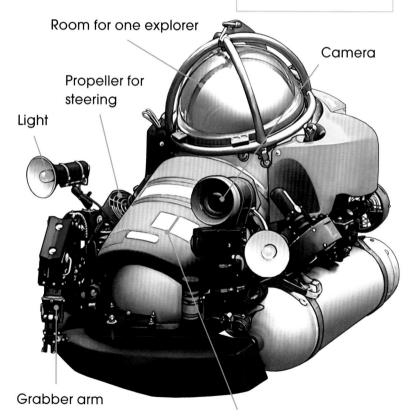

Room for one explorer

Camera

Propeller for steering

Light

Grabber arm

Thick, strong hull

Hydrofoil

Have you ever seen a boat with wings? A hydrofoil's wings are hidden underwater. As the boat speeds up, the wings lift the hull out of the water. This helps the boat to travel faster.

The underwater wings are called foils.

Hull

Foil

Strut

Only the foils are in the water

 # Ferry

Ferries are like buses on water. They carry passengers on short journeys, at regular times. Some ferries carry cars and lorries, too.

Look out for ferries of different shapes and sizes.

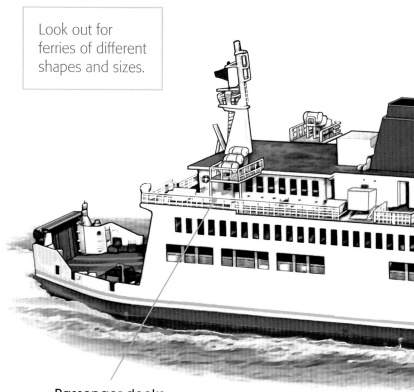

Passenger decks

This is a roll-on, roll-off ferry. It has huge doors so cars can drive on and off.

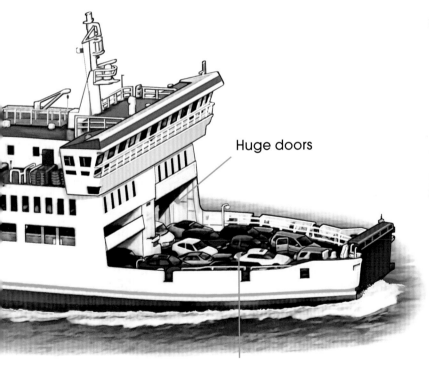

Huge doors

Car deck

Steamboat

A hundred years ago, many boats were powered by steam engines. You can see steamboats in museums. Some are still working.

Water is heated to make steam. The steam turns propellers or paddle wheels.

Funnel lets out steam from the engine

Paddle wheel

The paddles push against the water as the paddlewheel turns. The boat moves forwards.

Tall ship

Large ships with many sails are known as tall ships. They are built with traditional materials. Each sail has a different job. Some carry the ship along. Some are for steering.

This tall ship looks like an historic ship, but it has engines and computers onboard.

Masts

This tall ship has a crew of 69 people.

18 sails

Bowsprit

Containership

Slow-moving cargo ships carry goods and materials around the world. This ship carries goods inside steel boxes called containers. Cranes lift the containers on and off the ship quickly.

Some containers are carried in the hold. Others are stacked like bricks on deck.

Radar

Crew quarters

Containers

Hold

Tanker

Tankers carry oil, natural gas, and other fuels inside huge tanks. The hull has many layers to keep the cargo cool, and stop it from leaking into the sea.

It takes at least 15 minutes to bring this huge ship to a stop.

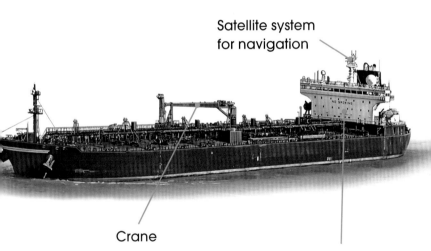

Satellite system for navigation

Crane

Bridge (ship's control centre)

Supertankers are the world's largest ships. Sometimes crew members use bicycles to travel around the decks.

Barge

Barges carry heavy loads, such as coal, or enormous objects. Ocean-going barges are much bigger than river barges.

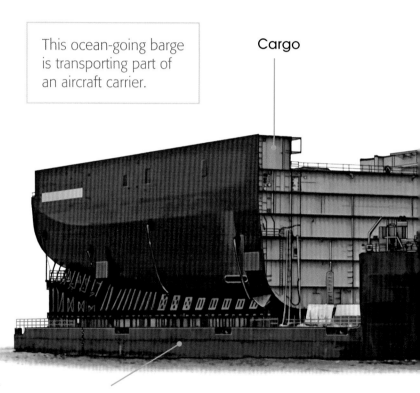

This ocean-going barge is transporting part of an aircraft carrier.

Cargo

Huge flat deck

Some barges have engines. Others are towed by tugboats.

Tugboat

Tugboats are small but very powerful. They can push and pull much bigger ships and boats. They do important jobs in ports and harbours.

Huge cargo ships cannot steer well in small spaces. Tugboats move them into the right place.

Wheelhouse

Hull

Towing line

Tugboats rescue ships that have broken down, and work as floating fire engines.

Cruise liner

This giant ship is a floating hotel. It carries thousands of passengers on holiday to far-away places.

Lifts carry passengers between decks.

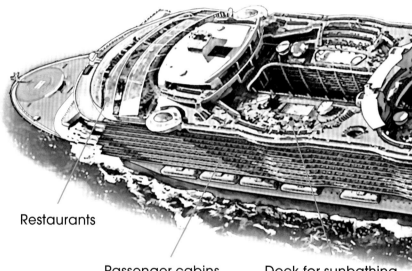

Restaurants

Passenger cabins

Deck for sunbathing

More than 1000 crew members look after the ship and its passengers.

Everything they need is onboard.

Children can visit a play zone with games, computers, and a splash pool.

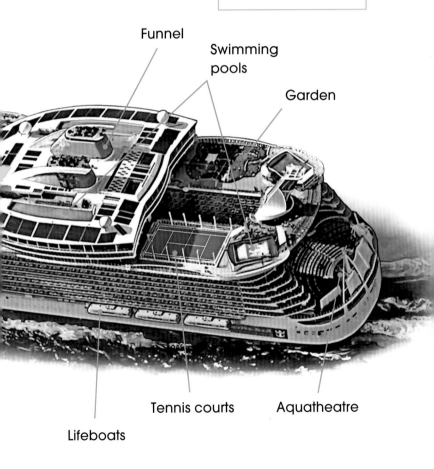

Funnel

Swimming pools

Garden

Lifeboats

Tennis courts

Aquatheatre

Icebreaker

Icebreakers can smash through thick ice on frozen seas. They clear a path for cargo ships and oil tankers, and carry supplies around the Arctic.

Big icebreakers can crush ice that is several metres thick.

Smooth, rounded bow

Strong hull

The bow slides up on to the ice. The ship's weight presses down on the ice, breaks it up, and pushes it out of the way.

Emergency services boat

Coastguards, police, and firefighters need boats to patrol the coast, and for emergency missions at sea. The boats carry equipment to do many different jobs.

This boat can speed to rescue sinking ships, and tow damaged ships back to land.

Folding arm

Platform for rescuing people

Searchlight

Water cannon

The engines pump seawater through cannons to fight fires.

Houseboat

This barge once carried cargo along rivers and canals. It has been changed into a floating home.

Some houseboats never move about. They are moored in one place.

Cabin with electricity supply

Deck

Passage to walk from bow to stern

There is a kitchen, living room, bathroom, and bedrooms on board.

Luxury yacht

Luxury yachts are built for comfortable trips at sea. They have bedrooms, bathrooms, and large rooms for eating and relaxing.

Personal watercraft and small boats are carried on board, for exploring coasts.

Some yachts even have swimming pools.

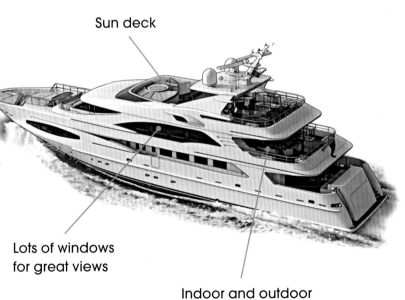

Sun deck

Lots of windows for great views

Indoor and outdoor eating areas

Rowing boat

People use oars to push rowing boats through the water. Different types of rowing boats are used for fun, transport, and racing.

Spot people rowing for fun on rivers and lakes.

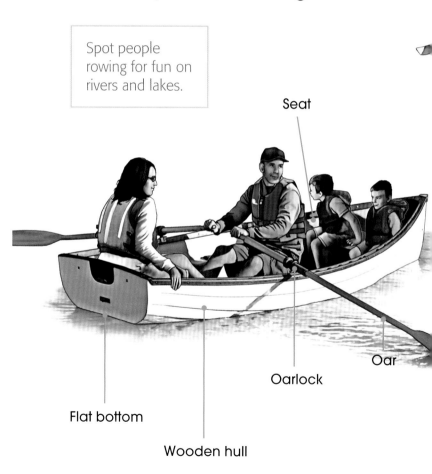

Seat

Flat bottom

Wooden hull

Oarlock

Oar

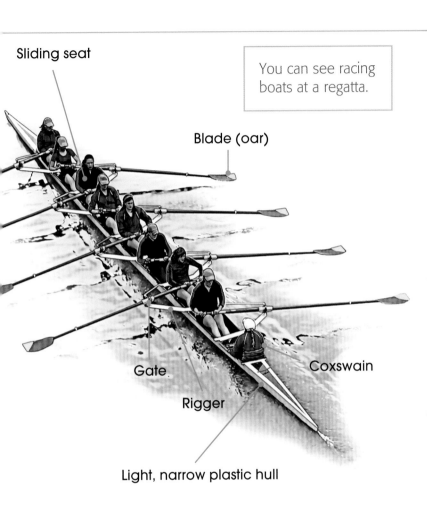

Sliding seat

You can see racing boats at a regatta.

Blade (oar)

Gate

Coxswain

Rigger

Light, narrow plastic hull

This racing boat has eight oarsmen. The coxswain steers the boat and tells the crew what to do.

# Hovercraft

Look out for hovercraft on water and land. They can travel from water straight onto the shore!

A giant fan blasts air downwards and traps a layer of air underneath the hovercraft. This lifts the hovercraft off the water or land.

Guard

Fan

Bendy rubber skirt traps a layer of air

The fan also pushes the hovercraft along on the cushion of air.

Useful words

bow front end of a boat or ship

bowsprit a pole that sticks out at the front of a ship. Some of the rigging is attached to it

deck a floor of a ship

engine a machine that burns fuel to make a ship or boat go

hull main body of a boat or ship

radar a system that uses radio waves to detect objects on or above water

regatta a series of boat races

rigging ropes and cables that hold up a mast

stern back end of a boat or ship

yacht boat used for pleasure or racing

Spotter's guide

How many of these ships and
boats have you seen? Tick
them when you spot them.

Sailing boat
page 6

Motorboat
page 7

Fishing trawler
page 8

Canoe
page 10

Chinese junk
page 17

Warship
page 18

Aircraft carrier
page 19

Historic ship
page 20

Inflatable boat
page 21

Submersible
page 22

Hydrofoil
page 23

Ferry
page 24

Steamboat
page 26

Tall ship
page 27

Containership
page 28

Tanker
page 29

Luxury yacht
page 37

Rowing boat
page 38

Racing rowing
boat
page 39

Hovercraft
page 40

Find out more

If you would like to find out more about ships and boats, you could visit a boat museum or a naval museum. These websites are a good place to start.

National Maritime Museum
www.rmg.co.uk

National Museum of the Royal Navy
www.royalnavalmuseum.org/

Merseyside Maritime Museum
www.liverpoolmuseums.org.uk/maritime/